Her Restless Heart

A Woman's Longing for Love and Acceptance

Leader Guide

A Faith and Fiction
BIBLE STUDY
with

BARBARA CAMERON

Lori Jones, Contributor

Abingdon Women
Nashville

HER RESTLESS HEART:
A WOMAN'S LONGING FOR LOVE AND ACCEPTANCE
LEADER GUIDE

Copyright © 2013 Abingdon Women

All rights reserved.

No part of this work may be reproduced or transmitted in any form or by any means, electronic or mechanical, including photocopying and recording, or by any information storage or retrieval system, except as may be expressly permitted by the 1976 Copyright Act or in writing from the publisher. Requests for permission can be addressed to Permissions, The United Methodist Publishing House, P.O. Box 801, 201 Eighth Avenue South, Nashville, TN 37202-0801, or emailed to permissions@umpublishing.org.

This book is printed on acid-free paper.
ISBN 978-1-4267-6173-7

Scriptures are taken from the Holy Bible, New International Version®, NIV®. Copyright ©1973, 1978, 1984, 2011 by Biblica, Inc.™ Used by permission of Zondervan. All rights reserved worldwide. www.zondervan.com. The "NIV" and "New International Version" are trademarks registered in the United States Patent and Trademark Office by Biblica, Inc.™

Scripture quotations marked ESV are from The Holy Bible, English Standard Version® (ESV®), copyright ©2001 by Crossway, a publishing ministry of Good News Publishers. Used by permission. All rights reserved.

Scripture quotations marked THE MESSAGE are from THE MESSAGE. Copyright © by Eugene H. Peterson 1993, 1994, 1995, 1996, 2000, 2001, 2002. Used by permission of NavPress Publishing Group.

Scripture quotations marked NKJV are taken from the New King James Version®. Copyright © 1982 by Thomas Nelson, Inc. Used by permission. All rights reserved.

Scripture quotations marked NCV are taken from the New Century Version®. Copyright © 2005 by Thomas Nelson, Inc. Used by permission. All rights reserved.

13 14 15 16 17 18 19 20 21 22—10 9 8 7 6 5 4 3 2 1

MANUFACTURED IN THE UNITED STATES OF AMERICA

Contents

Introduction 5

Week 1: The Hungry Heart 11

Week 2: The Wounded Heart 19

Week 3: The Insecure Heart 29

Week 4: The Reluctant Heart 37

Week 5: The Romantic Heart 45

Week 6: The Satisfied Heart 53

Notes 61

Introduction

Her Restless Heart is a six-week study that addresses our deepest desire as women: to find real and lasting love and acceptance. It acknowledges that we all want to experience love, full and complete, and to know that we are accepted for who we are—that we are free to be who we were made to be. Though we tend to look to people and things to fulfill this longing, we can never know true love and acceptance—or complete freedom—until we are able to rest in God's unconditional, all-encompassing love and to trust His plan for our lives.

This study invites us on a journey in which we will explore the depths of our hearts and allow God to satisfy our restlessness, offering us His love, acceptance, and peace. Together with the other women in your group, you will

- walk through your doubts and fears and find healing for your hearts—as well as our relationships;
- discover what it means to live a life of freedom by living in God's love;
- celebrate the God who is devoted to transforming us and blessing you beyond anything you ever dared to dream or imagine.

As leader, you will be shepherding the women in your group on this journey. It will be a time of learning, sharing, making discoveries, healing wounds, and growing into the women you are meant to be as you allow God to satisfy the longings that He alone can.

A Different Approach to Bible Study

What makes this study unique is that it uses Christian fiction as a backdrop to explore biblical themes. Through the characters in *Her Restless Heart* and their stories, you will learn how resting in God's great love for us frees us to experience His joy and peace. The hope is that this refreshing approach of combining Bible study with narrative storytelling not only will enrich and enhance your study of God's Word, but also will help you to understand better and apply what you're learning in your own lives as you relate to the characters and their experiences.

Everything you need to lead the study is provided in this leader guide and the DVD. Every group member will need a copy of the participant book. *Reading the novel is not*

required. However, anyone who enjoys reading and wants to read the novel in tandem with the study will find that this enhances the experience. Whether you and the women in your group choose to read the novel or only the excerpts and character sketches provided in the participant book, over the next six weeks you will come to know the characters in this story and the life challenges and healing journeys each experiences. The story revolves around Mary Katherine, a young Amish woman who is caught between the traditions of her faith and the pull of a different life. As she struggles with her restless heart and seeks to find her place in the world, she finds herself faced with difficult choices in love and in life. Her journey illuminates the universal restlessness and longing of the human heart for satisfaction and fulfillment. As you journey with Mary Katherine, you will be exploring the themes of desire, woundedness, insecurity, grace, decision making, relationships, community, transformation, new beginnings, and the goodness of God—all through a biblical framework encompassing both the Old and New Testaments.

About the Participant Book

The participant book contains a book summary of *Her Restless Heart*, along with several character sketches of the main characters in the novel and a glossary of Amish terms used in the novel. This introductory material is titled "Before You Begin." You will want to encourage participants to read this material before beginning the study, especially if they do not plan to read the novel.

Each week of study begins with a Scripture for the week and an excerpt from the novel, setting the stage for the five readings that follow. Each day's reading, which may be completed in approximately 20-30 minutes, follows this format:

Read God's Word	Focus Scripture for the day.
Reflect and Respond	Commentary on the focus Scripture and other selected Scriptures, personal application, and occasional excerpts from the novels—all offering insights related to the respective themes.
Talk to God	A prayer to use as is or to guide a personal time of prayer.
As You Go	Suggestion for the day—a question to ponder, Scripture to consider, or action to take.

Questions for reflection and response are sprinkled throughout the Reflect and Respond section. Participants will have the opportunity to share responses to some of these questions when you gather as a small group. Writing their thoughts in the space provided will prepare them for the weekly group sessions as well as capture the insights they are gaining on the journey.

Each week's readings conclude with a special "About the Amish" section, answering common questions about Amish customs, traditions, and practices.

Introduction

About This Leader Guide

This leader guide provides outlines for six group sessions, each structured for 60 minutes. If desired, you may extend the group sessions to 90 minutes by using the additional material provided at the end of each session outline (titled If You Have More Time).

Each session plan provides this format:

Getting Started (10 minutes)
A Few Minutes with Barbara (8-10 minutes)
Let's Talk About It (10 minutes)
Diving In (25 minutes)
In Closing (5 minutes)
If You Have More Time (30 additional minutes)

Getting Started provides ideas and suggestions for opening your time together and getting the conversation going. After this opening time, you will watch **A Few Minutes with Barbara**, a video interview providing background information and insights into the characters, stories, and themes of the novel as well as the weekly study themes. Then, **Let's Talk About It** gives participants the opportunity to respond to the video segment. Next comes **Diving In**, an interactive time of study and discussion focused on the week's readings in the participant book. Specific directions, comments, questions, and thoughts are provided to help you lead your group during this time. (Notations in parentheses—such as Day 1, Day 2, and so forth—indicate the day's reading in which a question may be found in the participant book.) You may read the material aloud where indicated or paraphrase this material in your own words. Feel free to adapt all of the material in this section as you wish to make it your own and meet the needs of your particular group. Finally, **In Closing** presents an activity and/or prayer to conclude your time together. (Note: If you are extending the time to 90 minutes, you may choose from the additional discussion questions and activities provided in **If You Have More Time**, using them before **In Closing**.)

Tips for Leading Your Group

Leading a group involves responsibilities as well as great rewards. To help make your experience as fruitful and rewarding as possible, here are a few helpful tips:

- Have a clear beginning and ending time for your group. Starting and ending on time shows members that their time and efforts to attend are respected.
- Meet in a comfortable place that encourages good conversation. Consider having light snacks and drinks to create a welcoming atmosphere.

- Be prepared to answer discussion questions first if it seems that others are slow to do so, but keep in mind that you should not do all the talking. Be okay with awkward pauses or moments of silence. Encourage others when they do respond.
- Because of the personal nature of this study, the recommended group size is 6-12 women. If your group has more than 12, you might want to watch the video segment together and divide into small groups for discussion of the study material.
- Be aware that some women in your group may have deep emotions and reactions to some of the material in this study. They may desire healing in deep places, and the hurts in their lives may be substantial. Demonstrate through your actions and words that it's okay if participants get emotional when discussing content. You're all in this together, and it's important that you foster a supportive environment for exploring the deep places where God is leading. Providing boxes of tissue can help to communicate a safe and open atmosphere in which showing emotions is allowed.

I am honored to walk alongside you as we travel this road together. I pray that God showers you and your group with His unconditional love and acceptance each step of the way.

Barbara Cameron

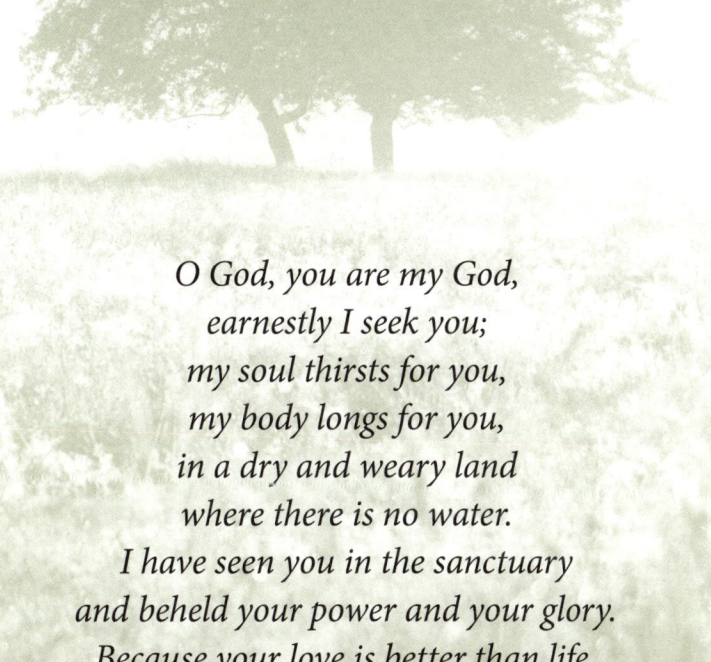

O God, you are my God,
earnestly I seek you;
my soul thirsts for you,
my body longs for you,
in a dry and weary land
where there is no water.
I have seen you in the sanctuary
and beheld your power and your glory.
Because your love is better than life,
my lips will glorify you.
I will praise you as long as I live,
and in your name I will lift up my hands.
My soul will be satisfied as with the richest of foods;
with singing lips my mouth will praise you.

Psalm 63:1-5

Week 1
The Hungry Heart

Getting Started (10 minutes)

- If your group is meeting together for the first time, have each person introduce herself by telling her name and something about herself (e.g., what she likes to do in her spare time; her favorite book, TV show, magazine; etc.). If your group has met previously, have each member share an area of her life in which God is challenging her right now.
- Take a few minutes to introduce the study. Explain that participants need to complete the readings for each week (found in the participant book) *prior to* the group session. Review the format of the group session (see the Introduction) and ask if there are any questions before you get started.
- Open with prayer, asking God to bless your time together.

A Few Minutes with Barbara (8-10 minutes)

Play the video for Week 1.

Let's Talk About It (10 minutes)

- Barbara suggests that Mary Katherine's restlessness is rooted in her need to know and believe that she is loved. In what ways do you think restlessness is connected to this need?
- Barbara talks about how women of all ages often experience restlessness because of busyness and a yearning deep within for something more. When have you experienced this sense of restlessness in your own life?
- Barbara shares how she finds peace and stillness by being alone and doing things she enjoys. What are some of the things that bring peace, stillness, and enjoyment in your life?
- Do you agree that the things we long for point us to the deepest desires of our hearts? Why or why not?
- What other points or insights from the video would you like to discuss with the group?

Notes

Her Restless Heart

Notes

Diving In (25 minutes)

Read Aloud

This week we have explored how our hearts are filled with longing, and we have seen that though our hearts long for many things, above all they long for love and acceptance. They long to trust and to be trusted, to be filled to capacity with peace and contentment. And though we search for fulfillment in the people and places around us, what our hearts truly cry out for is the complete love that only God can give.

- Have someone read aloud Genesis 2:15-18, 22; 3:1-7.

From the very beginning of time, we humans have struggled with the desire for *more*. More knowledge, more beauty, more pleasure, more power, more fulfillment.

Adam and Eve walked with God Himself in the most perfect environment possible. It was a breathtakingly beautiful place. God provided for their every need. They had companionship and important work. What more could they want?

But somewhere in the recesses of Eve's mind there was a question: *what if there is more?* A few words from a crafty serpent opened the floodgates of temptation, and an act of disobedience forever altered mankind's relationship with God.

Discuss

- What do you imagine the Garden of Eden looked like? How do you imagine its beauty affected the senses—what did it smell like, how did its fruit taste, what sounds would you have heard, what textures would you have felt, what beauty might your eyes have seen? (Day 1)

  Thoughts: Ask members to share details they imagine when they think about the Garden. Point to the fact that it was the most perfect environment imaginable.

- How does Genesis 3:7-13 describe how Adam and Eve reacted after they ate the fruit of the tree? What do you imagine was their immediate reaction—what might their thoughts have been? How do you think they viewed the Garden after that moment? (Day 1)

  Thoughts: After their rebellion, maybe it became a scary place, no longer beautiful and perfect, or maybe it was still perfect, but they could no longer enjoy it. Their longing for more, even though more wasn't possible, destroyed their world.

Read Aloud

Adam and Eve lived in a literal paradise, their every need met and their every want answered. But they were restless, and when faced with a life-changing decision, they succumbed to that restlessness and longing for more.

We aren't so different from Adam and Eve, are we? Our hearts and minds are filled with longings that we can rarely name, but that we feel down deep in the core of our being. We're unsatisfied with the world around us. We're frustrated with our relationships, which regularly fail to meet our expectations. We struggle to enjoy the work of our hands. We feel trapped by all the freedoms we're supposed to enjoy.

What do we really want? Why are we so unsatisfied?

Some days we may experience a strong, almost physical restlessness that results in anger or frustration. But most often we live with a quiet restlessness. We may have a vague sense that something's wrong in this life, but we aren't sure what it is exactly or how to fix it. The ambiguity and uncertainty can cause us to question things—our faith, our marriages, our work, our environments—in a desperate search to find the broken piece and repair it or change it altogether.

Notes

Discuss

- Though she enjoys the fruitful work of her hands and rich relationships with the women in her life, Mary Katherine is restless in Paradise, Pennsylvania. She isn't sure that she fits in with the community around her and is unsure she can live up to their expectations, but at the same time she desperately wants to find her place in the world. Naomi jokes that Mary Katherine was "born restless." Do you think that certain personalities are prone to restlessness? Would you consider yourself a restless personality? If so, in what ways? (Day 2)
- What are some reasons that you think we, as women, are often restless? What emotional and cultural factors do you think contribute to this restlessness? (Day 2)
  Thoughts: Answers here can vary widely. Sometimes our busyness and the many roles we play in life can cause us to feel restless. Sometimes striving for perfection can result in restlessness. Sometimes the virtual world around us—full of social media, blogs, and websites—can encourage comparison, leading us to think that we aren't enough in one area or another, resulting in restlessness.

Read Aloud

In many ways, our culture is designed to keep us restless and unsatisfied. Constant advertisements sell us on the idea that something else is better than what we have. Our economy is fueled by competition and comparison. Being complacent—content—is frowned upon. The fear that being content will make us unproductive keeps us striving and working harder and harder. The idea of rest and stillness seems indulgent and lazy.

Though it seems as if our modern-day culture conspires to keep us restless and wanting more, our present dilemmas are nothing new to the condition of the human heart. Consider the Old Testament book of Ecclesiastes. The author, King Solomon, was a king of great renown. The son of Israel's beloved King David, Solomon had restored the people's faith by building an amazing temple to be a place of worship and a home for the

Notes

Ark of the Covenant (also known as God's presence). He was an extremely successful king by anyone's standards, and the world was seemingly at his fingertips. Solomon had everything that a man could acquire. And yet he was restless.

- Have someone read aloud Ecclesiastes 1:1-10.

Ecclesiastes reads like a diary of sorts, chronicling Solomon's pursuit of fulfillment, meaning, and joy. Wisdom—check! Success—check! Wealth—check! Solomon had all those things in spades, and yet he found that nothing he could acquire or attain could give him the deep and satisfying joy that he found when he finally realized he could rest in God's love, provision, and authority. Pursuing anything else, he said, is like "chasing the wind" (Ecclesiastes 1:17).

Centuries after Solomon lived, a young man named Augustine found himself struggling with the same frustrations and fruitless searches Solomon experienced. After living a life devoted first to seeking pleasure and then to seeking wisdom through various philosophical pursuits, Augustine finally discovered that a life of devotion to God and reveling in his status as God's child was the only thing that could truly satisfy. In his classic book *Confessions*, he wrote, "Thou hast formed us for Thyself, and our hearts are restless till they find rest in Thee."[2]

When Mary Katherine discovers her gift for weaving, she finds fulfillment in her work and receives much encouragement about its quality and beauty from customers, her grandmother, and her cousins. Although she is able to find joy and some peace in that area of her life, it does not fulfill a deeper desire—to experience unconditional love and acceptance from her family and her community. This desire, of course, is only a shadow of her heart's true and greatest desire, which is to know and experience the unconditional love and acceptance of God. Like Solomon, she discovers that the work of her hands cannot fulfill the deep desires of her heart.

Discuss

- How do you identify with Solomon's frustration in finding meaning in his life? Have you faced similar struggles of your own? (Day 3) Do you identify with Mary Katherine's frustration? How?
- Is anyone willing to share her answer to this question: What do you most desire in your life? (Day 3)

Read Aloud

- Have someone read aloud Proverbs 13:12.

What both King Solomon and Saint Augustine discovered through their experience and disappointment was that choosing to trust and live in God's love is the ultimate source of life and fulfillment for our hearts. Anything else will be less than what we've hoped for, and realizing less than what we've hoped for indeed makes the heart sick.

God's gift of complete love and acceptance required no small sacrifice. John 3:16 says, "For God so loved the world that he gave his one and only Son, that whoever believes in him shall not perish but have eternal life." God sent His Son, Jesus, to Earth to become the sacrifice for our sins and pave the way for us to have an intimate relationship with Him. Trusting in that sacrifice and reveling in our state as God's beloved children is the only way our hearts will find fulfillment during our short time here on Earth. He is the only One who can fulfill the complete desires of our hearts.

God's salvation and grace is a gift to us—there is nothing we can do to earn the gift, and there is nothing we can add to or take away from it. All we need to do is open our hands to the gift of His love and accept it—gratefully and eagerly. It is a perfect gift, and in His love we will find rest for our hungry hearts.

Notes

Discuss

- Second Peter 1:3 says, "[God's] divine power has given us everything we need for life and godliness." God has given us His love and His grace—everything that we need to fulfill the deepest longings of our hearts. So why do you think we still tend to have restless hearts? (Day 4)

    Thoughts: Often we let our own doubts and fears cloud the truth and keep us from fully experiencing what God has given us. We erroneously think we need to do more for God in order to be truly accepted by Him. Because we tend to think we must earn God's love, we're often afraid to let go and fully trust Him because we're afraid we'll mess it up.

Read Aloud

A strong, sensitive, and independent young woman, Mary Katherine wants to be loved for who she is. She finds that she doesn't neatly fit into the mold that many women in her community embody; she wants to be loved and accepted for her own strengths, not just because she can be a good farm wife. In a sense, we are all like Mary Katherine—we all want to know that we are not alone, that we are understood and accepted, that we are loved—in spite of and because of all of the doubts and fears and hopes and dreams inside of us that make us who we are.

In many ways, our lives are defined by the longings of our hearts, and if we are willing to take a brave look at how we respond to those longings, they will point us to the deepest desires of our hearts. If we long to be restored, we might pursue perfection here on Earth. If we long to be loved at all costs, we might be willing to morph into whatever form it takes to get love from someone else. If we long for peace, we might choose to fade into the background of our relationships, hoping not to cause any trouble or rock the boat. If we long for passion, we might search out things that give us a temporary thrill or

Notes

excitement. If we long for acceptance, we might become workaholics to gain approval and appreciation.

Our hearts are complex places, and at times our longings can seem overwhelming and even consuming. But God Himself formed our hearts and our minds and gave us complex emotions and thoughts. The longings themselves are not bad; in fact, they are beautiful, for when we take a prayerful look at the deepest desires of our hearts, we find that everything our hearts long for can be found in God.

God can use the deepest longings and groanings of our hearts to point us back to Him and His love.

Discuss

- Read the following verses. What does each have to say about how God meets the deepest desires of our hearts? (Day 5)
    o Ephesians 1:3-6
    Thoughts: God has given us life; He has brought us into His family.
    o Zephaniah 3:17
    Thoughts: He delights in us for who we are—His creation, His children.

Read Aloud

God, our Creator and Father, has given us life and brought us into His family. He has focused His love on us, adopted us, and given us indescribable mercy and grace, lavishing His love over us and delighting in us. How amazing to know that every desire of our hearts is fulfilled through Him!

In Closing (5 minutes)

As you close your time together today, lead your group into a time of quiet reflection as you read aloud the following verses, pausing after each one to give participants time to reflect and pray:

> *Search me, God, and know my heart;*
> *test me and know my anxious thoughts.*
> *See if there is any offensive way in me,*
> *and lead me in the way everlasting.*
> Psalm 139:23-24

[God's] divine power has given us everything we need for life and godliness.
2 Peter 1:3a

*Give thanks to the L*ORD*, for he is good;*
his love endures forever....
*Let them give thanks to the L*ORD *for his unfailing love*
and his wonderful deeds for mankind,
for he satisfies the thirsty
and fills the hungry with good things.

Psalm 107:1, 8-9

Notes

Close in prayer, thanking God that He is more than enough to satisfy our hungry hearts. Ask for God's gentle voice to speak into each heart and to reveal the ways in which we seek to find our source of love and acceptance in anything other than Him. Pray that through this study we would learn how His perfect love and grace can fill our hearts and our lives with peace and joy.

If You Have More Time
(30 additional minutes; use before In Closing)

Choose from the following:
- Invite participants to talk more about their expectations for this study.
  - *Discuss:* What do you think it means to be loved and accepted? What do you hope to learn or gain from this study?
- Explore how we can find comfort in God.
  - Note that when Martin Luther was discouraged, he would say, "Come, let us sing the forty-sixth psalm."[1] Have someone read aloud Psalm 46 and discuss how it teaches us to take comfort in God when everything around us seems dim and threatening.
  - *Discuss:* Do you pursue peace, rest, and stillness in your own life? If so, how? If not, what takes precedence over those things in your life? How are those priorities affecting your life? What do you think God means when He tells the psalmist to "be still, and know that I am God"? (Day 2)
- Talk about times when it seems that God is silent.
  - *Read aloud:* As Mary Katherine's decision to join the church weighs heavy on her, she begins to doubt that God is listening to her. Like Mary Katherine, we may sometimes wonder if God is silent because we are doing something wrong or because we don't have enough faith to warrant His attention. But Scripture repeatedly tells us that God is listening and that He hears the cries of His children. He will not leave us stranded and alone. He is committed to our good, and He desires for us to follow Him.
  - *Discuss:* What do Psalm 34:17, 1 John 5:14, and Hebrews 13:5 say about God's attention toward His children? (Day 4)

Week 2
The Wounded Heart

Notes

Note: This week's discussion about woundedness and hurt can be a heavy and complicated subject. As you discuss the subject matter for this group session, be sensitive to participants' emotions and responses. Don't be afraid of silence or strong emotion, but strive to maintain the most safe and supportive atmosphere possible for your group. This is not a time and place for airing grievances against others. If the conversation verges into gossipy territory, redirect the group gently.

Getting Started (10 minutes)

- Ask the group one or both of the following questions:
   o Are you reading (or have you read) *Her Restless Heart*? If so, what do you like most about it? Which characters do you most connect with?
   o What is one of your favorite childhood memories?
- Open with prayer, asking God to bless your time together.

A Few Minutes with Barbara (8-10 minutes)

Play the video for Week 2.

Let's Talk About It (10 minutes)

- Barbara talks about how Mary Katherine has been wounded by her father and how she tries to honor him without being hurtful in return. When have you been wounded by a critical person, and how did you respond?
- What does Barbara say about why it is so important for Mary Katherine to learn to forgive her father and herself? What happens when we hold grudges?
- Barbara shares about the power of encouraging words in Mary Katherine's life. How have the encouraging words of others played an important role in your own life?
- Barbara shares how her wounds, including those inflicted by a critical parent, led her to find healing. Why do you think our wounds often lead us to God? How has this been true in your own life?
- What other points or insights from the video would you like to discuss with the group?

Her Restless Heart

Notes

Diving In (25 minutes)

Read Aloud

During this week, we discovered how the characters in *Her Restless Heart*—and specifically Mary Katherine—are learning to deal with the hurts in their lives. As we see in the characters' lives, life has a way of shaping us, and not always through the ways we would choose. The battlefields of our lives can leave us battered and scarred, weary from the fight. But out of the struggle come triumph and a quiet knowledge that our scars can be beautiful reminders that there is a bigger story only God can tell.

For as long as she can remember, Mary Katherine has experienced pain and rejection in her father's presence. Whether assaulted by his biting, scathing words or suffering through his disapproving silences, Mary Katherine's heart and spirit have been wounded by her father's actions and attitude. Though she finds peace and joy in being in her grandmother's home and shop, the weight of those wounds still affects how she lives her life.

In William Faulkner's novel *Requiem for a Nun*, one of the characters says, "The past is never dead. It's not even past."[1] Doesn't that statement often feel true? Though time moves on and we try to move past the wounds that life has given us, at times it seems that our present is hijacked by our past and we are once again consumed with the hurts and offenses that have shaped our lives.

We live in a fallen world, and all of us have been wounded in one way or another. We all carry the scars of living and of battles fought. Some of us have been shaped by dramatic, life-altering events, while others have been shaped in quieter, subtler ways. Nevertheless, we are all battle-weary warriors, and the weavings of our lives leave marks on us, big or small.

Discuss

- Have there been events or relationships in your life that have inflicted wounds upon your heart and spirit? How have they affected your life to this point? How have you considered God in light of those events or relationships—have you believed He was present during those times, or distant? How has this affected your relationship with God? (Day 1)

  Note: In order to open up discussion, you may want to begin by sharing about a time in your life when you felt wounded. If no one else volunteers to share, don't push the question. This could be sensitive for some group members.

Read Aloud

We all remember those formative moments in our lives when we've felt rejected, confused, or hurt by another person's actions. At some point or another, someone has made us feel as if we were not good enough, pretty enough, smart enough, worthy enough, fill-in-the-blank enough. Some of those instances were probably more trivial, and we eventually laughed them off, while others may have been so serious that we have dealt with their repercussions for years. Either way, these incidents can make us feel unworthy of love and acceptance and lead us to make choices that cause us additional grief and harm. John 8:2-11 tells the story of a woman caught in a desperate state.

Notes

- Have someone read aloud John 8:2-11.

We do not know this woman's name or how she looked or what her past was like, but we can only imagine how humiliated and worthless she must have felt as she stood before Jesus. Caught in the act of adultery, her shame must have run so deep that she could barely breathe. (Not to mention that she was facing a death sentence for her mistake.) We will never know what events, relationships, and experiences in this woman's life led her to make the choices she made. We will never know how her situation was manipulated and exploited for others' gain. What we do know is this: Jesus had compassion for her and offered her not condemnation, but love and freedom. He offered her a second chance at life.

As we see in John 8 and in countless places throughout the Gospels, Jesus offers grace and love for our hurting hearts and messy situations. When we are heavy with pain and guilt, when we can barely lift our heads to look Him in the eye, Jesus says to come to Him and He will carry our burdens.

Discuss

- What is your initial reaction when you hear this story of this woman? What emotions does it stir within you? (Day 2)
- Mary Katherine's *Englisch* friend, Jamie, finds herself in a hard situation when she thinks she might be pregnant with her boyfriend's baby. Jamie, like Mary Katherine, has experienced conflict with and rejection from her own father, and she is living on her own at a young age. Knowing this, how do you think Jamie's past might have influenced her present circumstances and the mistakes she has made? (Day 2)
- Why do you think Jesus told the woman to go and leave her life of sin? How was He addressing her view of her identity through this command? (Day 2)
  Thoughts: Jesus wanted her to know that she was worth more—that He valued her more—than the choices she was making. He wanted her to see herself as forgiven and freed from those things that had beat her down.
- What do you think Jesus wanted to teach everyone gathered there that day about forgiveness? (Day 2)
  Thoughts: Jesus demonstrated that forgiveness is important—essential to transformation—and that He gave it freely.

Her Restless Heart

Read Aloud

The word *father* conjures up many different thoughts and emotions. When some people hear *father*, words such as *love, protection, gentleness,* and *strength* come to mind. For others, all they can think is *fear, abandonment, judgment, rejection,* and *pain.*

Mary Katherine's father, Isaac, was clearly the head of his family. And though he worked hard and provided for his family's basic needs, his emotional and spiritual leadership of his family was certainly lacking. His wife and daughter were diminished in his domineering presence, and their spirits suffered from his general displeasure and criticism.

Though Mary Katherine doesn't intend for her view of her earthly father to interfere with her perception of her heavenly Father, doubt and lack of trust are seeping into her relationship with God. She finds herself talking less and less to God, and though she still wants a relationship with Him, in some ways she feels abandoned by God because He didn't rescue her from her unhappy family situation when she was younger.

Discuss

- How do you think Mary Katherine's view of God has been affected by her relationship with her own father? Which of her father's characteristics might Mary Katherine be projecting onto God? (Day 3)

  Thoughts: She has trouble trusting God and believing that He has a good plan for her life because she prayed for God to change her unhappy home life, but it continues to be a struggle. She is afraid that she will disappoint God like she has disappointed her father, and she is afraid of making choices that will keep God from truly accepting her. She wants to please God but perhaps wonders if that will ever happen.

- How has your relationship with your earthly father shaped your life? How has your relationship with your earthly father shaped your view of God? (Day 3)

Read Aloud

It doesn't take more than a brief look at the local news or newspaper to see that there are many fathers who are not doing a good job of loving and caring for their children. We've all heard the stories; some of us have experienced them firsthand. That makes the picture of fatherhood that Jesus describes in Luke 15 even sweeter.

In this story, the parable of the prodigal son, we see the remarkable picture of a humble, loving father and how he responded in a gut-wrenching situation. His youngest son had tired of living in his father's house and wanted to go out into the world to live his own life. In those days, a son asking for his inheritance was essentially saying to his father, "Why should I wait until you're dead to get my money?" It was a shameful, embarrassing situation for the family to have such a disrespectful and irresponsible son.

But when the son recklessly squandered what he'd been given and was forced to return to his father, the story takes an unexpected turn. His father looks out over the fields and sees a lone figure limping toward home. Maybe he had been watching, waiting expectantly for his son's return all along. But when he finally sees him, he starts running toward his disrespectful, ungrateful son. He *runs*. This is not the posture of a prideful man intending to punish one who had shamed him. This is not the posture of a man who has had his feelings hurt and plans on turning a cold shoulder. This is the posture of grace.

The father runs to his son and embraces him, eager to restore this prodigal and give him more than he could ever dare to ask for. This is a picture of our God. This is a picture of our Father. How sweet to know that God is the Good Father, committed to our restoration. He is not proud or self-protecting. He is not wounded or vindictive.

God our Father heals and protects. He embraces and rejoices. He guides with love and mercy. He offers us redemption, freely and completely.

Notes

Discuss

- Why do you think Jesus chose to teach this parable? What do you think He was trying to say to those who were listening that day? How is He speaking to you through this story? (Day 3)

Read Aloud

Our families represent the baselines of our lives, the starting points from which we gain understanding and experience about the world and other people. From them we are taught to have a certain perspective and to accept basic fundamentals about how life should be lived and how other people should be treated. Mary Katherine's early life experiences in her own family taught her that being a child (and being a female) landed her firmly in the place of being a second-class citizen, and that her value depended on what she could do for her family.

As Mary Katherine grew and her perspective expanded, she began to question her parents' example and the way her father treated her and her mother, Miriam. Receiving encouragement and kind guidance from other parental figures, such as her grandmother, Mary Katherine soon found that her view of the world did not match up with her parents' view of the world, and she chose to escape their home for an environment that encouraged her natural talents and abilities. Though Mary Katherine left her parents' home, she soon found out that she couldn't totally escape the effect their attitudes had had upon her life, and so we find her struggling with doubt, fear, and insecurity about her future.

Discuss

- How would you describe your relationship with your parents? What baseline for living life did you receive from them? (Day 4)

Her Restless Heart

Notes

- When Mary Katherine and her father, Isaac, do not see eye to eye, he often quotes Exodus 20:12 to her: "Honour thy father and thy mother: that thy days may be long upon the land which the Lord thy God giveth thee" (KJV). Why do you think he quotes this verse to his daughter? What do you think is his perspective on this verse? Do you think this perspective is correct? Why or why not? (Day 4)
  Thoughts: Isaac seems to believe that this verse gives him complete authority as a parent and serves as proof that he should never be challenged or questioned. Though, clearly, God does command us to respect our parents (the command appears again in Ephesians 6:1-3), this command is not intended to give parents the right to abuse or dominate their children.
- Another command, in Ephesians 6:4, says, "Fathers, don't exasperate your children by coming down hard on them" (*THE MESSAGE*). Why is it significant that both of these commands—*honor your father and mother and don't exasperate your children*—are included in the Bible? What do they point both parents and children to do? (Day 4)
  Thoughts: God wants us to have respect and love for one another, to treat one another with gentleness and patience, and not to control or manipulate one another.

Read Aloud

No parent who has ever walked this Earth has been perfect; likewise, there are no perfect children. We are all sinful, imperfect beings who like to live life on our own terms, and we will make mistakes—and make them often. That is why God encourages us to love and respect these people who play such a huge role in our lives. We are to love and respect each other not because we always deserve it, but because God commands us to love as He loves.

Likewise, God calls us to forgive. When Leah tells Mary Katherine that she needs to forgive her father for his words and attitudes, Mary Katherine is surprised that her grandmother would suggest *she* be the one to offer forgiveness. After all the hurt he has caused Mary Katherine, she can't imagine that offering forgiveness to her father will change their relationship or his attitude.

As a child, it's easy to blame your parent for anything that you consider to be a failing. Maybe there was a time that you felt a parent didn't give you enough love or acceptance, or at least didn't show it when you needed it. But then when you become a parent yourself, you see how impossible a job it is—that you can't be everything for that child, and that most of the time you don't know what you're doing anyway.

Sometimes we forget that our parents did not emerge from the womb as the people they are today. They, too, have been shaped by the events and relationships in their lives, and they have their own scars to prove it. And though it can be hard to have compassion and see them as complete people—and not just our parents—perhaps that is just the kind of gentleness that God asks us to extend to them.

Discuss

- How might choosing to live with a spirit of forgiveness toward her father—which involves learning to love him as he is, with all his own baggage and failings—change the way Mary Katherine sees him? (Day 4)
  Thoughts: With God's help, choosing to live in forgiveness can help Mary Katherine to see others with God's eyes of compassion and love and to realize that her father has his own wounds to contend with.
- How can looking to God for love and acceptance—instead of looking to her father for those things—play an important part in changing Mary Katherine's view of her father and of herself? (Day 4)
  Thoughts: Relying on God as the Perfect Father and as her complete source of love and acceptance can free Mary Katherine to love as He loves. She no longer has to rely on her earthly father to fill those needs, but she can realize how much she is loved for who she is and was created to be by her Heavenly Father. She no longer has to carry the burden of trying to please her earthly father.

Notes

In Closing (5 minutes)

Close in prayer, thanking God for His ability to heal all our wounds and hurts. Ask God to show you how to forgive others for the hurts they have caused, and to give you His eyes to see others as He does. Thank Him for fighting for your healing, for being your champion, and for being a perfect Father Who lavishes love and grace upon His children.

If You Have More Time
(30 additional minutes; use before In Closing)

Choose from the following:
- Explore how God is with us through every battle we face in life, regardless of what it might be.
  o *Read aloud*: In the Old Testament, we read about the story of Moses and his people, the Israelites. Enslaved by the Egyptians for four hundred years, the beaten-down Israelites had suffered a cruel system of prejudice and marginalization under their masters. So when God sent Moses to lead them out of slavery, they were wary and afraid. Even so, they still followed Moses out of slavery in Egypt and into the desert and an unknown future. Their bravery did not last long, though, when they heard that Pharaoh and his army were pursuing them, and their resolve quickly dissolved into panic and fear.
  o Have someone read aloud Exodus 14:10-14. Acknowledge that just as the Lord fought for the Israelites and rescued them from the Egyptians, so God is present in every battle of our lives and is fighting for us. Just as God did not abandon the

Notes

Israelites, so He will not abandon us. Affirm that God will fight for our hearts and for our healing, and He will win the battle. We know this because of the testimony of God's faithfulness in the Bible as well as through the ages.

- o *Discuss:* Moses told the people, "The LORD will fight for you, and you have only to be silent" (Exodus 14:14 ESV). Why do you think he told them to be silent? (Day 1)

  Thoughts: So they would stop grumbling and complaining and trust God; so they would know that God had it all under control, on His own.

- o *Discuss:* Do you have trouble being silent sometimes and letting God work? How might being silent sometimes (either in word or in action) allow God to work in our lives? Do you sense or see God fighting for healing in your life? If so, in what areas? How are you responding to Him?

• Consider the importance of spoken words.
  - o Acknowledge that words seep into our hearts and minds and comprise the voices of encouragement or judgment that we hear over and over again in our minds.
  - o Point out that although Mary Katherine sometimes hears the negative voice of her father in her life, she also hears many words of encouragement from others who surround her. *Discuss:* Which characters give Mary Katherine encouragement, and why are these encouraging words so important in Mary Katherine's life? (Day 1)?
  - o Read aloud the following verses:

    "For I know the plans I have for you," declares the Lord, "plans to prosper you and not to harm you, plans to give you hope and a future. Then you will call on me and come and pray to me, and I will listen to you. You will seek me and find me when you seek me with all your heart."
    Jeremiah 29:11-13

    "Do not let your hearts be troubled. You believe in God; believe also in me. My Father's house has many rooms; if that were not so, would I have told you that I am going there to prepare a place for you? And if I go and prepare a place for you, I will come back and take you to be with me that you also may be where I am. You know the way to the place where I am going."
    John 14:1-4

    "I have told you these things, so that in me you may have peace. In this world you will have trouble. But take heart! I have overcome the world."
    John 16:33

Keep your lives free from the love of money and be content with what you have, because God has said,

> *"Never will I leave you;*
> *never will I forsake you."*

Hebrews 13:5

What do you hear God saying to you through these verses? (Day 5)

Notes

Week 3
The Insecure Heart

Notes

Getting Started (10 minutes)

- Ask the group the following question:
  - Do you have an unusual (or hidden) talent? What is it, and how did you discover you had it?
- Open with prayer, asking God to bless your time together.

A Few Minutes with Barbara (8-10 minutes)

Play the video for Week 3.

Let's Talk About It (10 minutes)

- Barbara talks about why Mary Katherine struggles with identity and self-worth. Why do you think that seeking her father's approval holds Mary Katherine back from discovering who she is?
- Barbara explores how Mary Katherine's relationship with her father influences her relationship with God. How has your relationship with your own father affected or influenced your relationship with God?
- Barbara gives us some insights into the character of Isaac, Mary Katherine's father. She suggests that although he comes across as cold and uncaring, this is not how he truly is. What would you say we can learn about Isaac—and others who are outwardly harsh and critical—from his behavior?
- Barbara talks about the symbolic nature of Mary Katherine's gift of weaving. How is it more than just a part of her creative self? Do you have a gift that plays a significant part in your life?
- Barbara suggests that the novel shows us what we can gain from our friendships with other women, especially those in a God-centered community. How is Mary Katherine's life impacted by her relationship with other women? How has your own life been impacted by relationships with women of faith?
- What other points or insights from the video would you like to discuss with the group?

Notes

Diving In (25 minutes)

Read Aloud

Though we sing hymns about God's powerful and complete love for us, and we quote Scriptures about His unending grace, if we are honest, we must admit that often our insecurities and fears overwhelm us and keep us from understanding and claiming just how much we are loved by God. So we try harder, and harder still, until we are defeated, exhausted, and hopeless. It seems that we can never do enough or be enough.

Like Mary Katherine, many of us have struggled at some point in our lives with issues related to identity and self-worth. With the cultural messages and pressures we face as women today, most of us have questioned at one time or another whether we measure up. We find ourselves thinking that we should do more or be more. Sometimes the mythical list of what we *should* be doing seems never ending. No wonder even the most self-assured of us sometimes question ourselves and our abilities!

When we find ourselves discouraged or disappointed, perhaps our problem is not that we need more *self*-esteem but that we need to be filled with *God*-esteem—something beyond anything we can attain on our own. A first step is to take a close look at *where* we're investing ourselves—and to what benefit.

Discuss

- In Isaiah 55:2, God gives us some clues to find where we are placing our hope and search for identity. He says, "Why spend money on what is not bread, and your labor on what does not satisfy?" Based on this verse, what is our "money"? What is our "labor"? (Day 1)
  Thoughts: Time, energy, expectations, resources.
- When you consider where you are placing your time, energy, resources, and expectations (also known as your "money" and your "labor"), what conclusions do you come to about where you tend to find your identity? (Day 1)

Read Aloud

All of the things we tend to invest our lives in—our families, our work, our relationships, our communities—are *good things*. They are certainly worth our time and attention, and God can use us to spread His love in these areas. But if we are looking to these things to give us worth and identity, they will fall short. They cannot satisfy our deepest desires. Our search will be never ending—and frustrating—if we try to find our identity and worth in these things.

- Have someone read aloud Isaiah 55:1.

Have you ever gone to a store and tried to buy something with no money? It's not likely that scenario worked out in your favor. Our whole economic system is based on currency—exchanging money for goods. This is a system that we understand from a very young age and adhere to throughout our lives. It's just the way things are done.

So, what does God mean when He says, "You who have no money, come, buy and eat! Come, buy wine and milk without money and without cost" (Isaiah 55:1b)? What is He trying to tell us?

God, speaking through the prophet Isaiah, invites anyone who is thirsty or hungry to come to "the waters" and be satisfied. Throughout his book, Isaiah often describes God's kingdom and salvation in terms of an abundance of water, and the images of wine and milk represent symbols of complete satisfaction and comfort. He beckons us to come freely and partake without any way to pay. Titus 3:5 says, "[God] saved us, not because of righteous things we had done, but because of his mercy. He saved us through the washing of rebirth and renewal by the Holy Spirit."

Notes

Discuss

- Have you ever felt that you had to earn God's favor? If so, how? (Day 2)
- What does Romans 3:23-24 tell us about our ability to earn God's favor? (Day 2) *Thoughts*: It's impossible to earn it. God's grace is a complete gift.
- For many years, Mary Katherine has been frustrated in her efforts to earn her father's affection and favor. Do you think that struggle has influenced how she feels about God and earning His favor? If so, how? How can you identify with her struggles? (Day 2)

Read Aloud

When it comes to our salvation, fulfillment, and identity as children of God, we have gone to the store with no money. There is no currency—wealth, abilities, strengths, good works—we can offer that could buy our redeemed status. Our precious worth was graciously bought on our behalf by Jesus' sacrifice and given to us by God.

The poet Macrina Wiederkehr wrote:

> *O God*
> *help me believe*
> *the truth about myself—*
> *no matter how beautiful it is!*[1]

Discuss

- Take a few minutes to reflect on these words. What do you think she is saying? How do her words encourage and challenge you? (Day 2)

Her Restless Heart

Notes

Thoughts: We are loved and redeemed—the work has been done! Sometimes this is hard for us to accept; it all seems too good to be true. So, often we keep trying to work for our salvation.

- How does believing the beautiful truth of God's gift of love and grace speak to your sense of self-worth? (Day 2)

Thoughts: Psalm 139 talks about how God has uniquely crafted each of us from the inside out, and how He has a great purpose for our lives. He is the Author of our lives, and He loved us so much that He was willing to send His Son, Jesus, to give us life and to restore us. Our value is immeasurable in His eyes.

Read Aloud

The early Christian church in Corinth had its issues, just as our modern-day churches do. We don't know all the ins and outs of their struggles, but Paul's first letter to them gives us some insight into their struggles. As the Corinthian church attempted to find its way, some members had apparently become imbalanced in their thinking, believing that those members who spoke in tongues were more exalted or spiritual than those who didn't. The issue was important to Paul.

- Have someone read aloud 1 Corinthians 12.

As members of the body of Christ, we each play a vital role in God's work here on Earth. Though we constantly tend to compare ourselves to others and try to "measure up" to determine our worth, there is sweet relief and reassurance in knowing that God has created each of us with specific and individualized gifts, strengths, and skills, and that He wants us to use them in service to the church and one another.

Discuss

- What are your particular gifts and strengths? How do you feel about them? (Day 3)
- How have others in the church responded to your gifts in the past? Have you received encouragement for those gifts, or have you felt that your gifts were inferior to others? How has the response of others affected how you use your gifts? (Day 3)
- Read Psalm 139:13-14. How does it make you feel to know that God has created every inch of your personality—that your gifts, strengths, and weaknesses were handcrafted for you alone? (Day 3)
- Though Mary Katherine hasn't found much support from her parents for her weaving, God slowly begins to show her how her she can use her abilities to weave and teach to touch other people's lives. In what ways do you think Mary Katherine's gifts, though not of the standard farm variety, can encourage and enrich her community? How can you use your gifts to serve your own community? (Day 3)

In Closing (5 minutes)

Close in prayer, asking God to give you eyes to see where you are trusting your own work and abilities to give you value and worth. Ask Him to help you understand the value of His gift of grace, which is undeserved but freely given. Pray that you will have eyes to see where God has uniquely gifted you, and that God would lead you to opportunities where you can use your gifts to serve and enrich the community around you.

Notes

If You Have More Time
(30 additional minutes; use before In Closing)

Choose from the following:
- Consider what happens when we are unable to accept God's love.
  - Explain that when we cannot accept God's love and see ourselves as whole and redeemed in light of God's grace, we are unable to love others as God wants us to love them. Make the following points: 1) When we seek to earn our worthiness through our actions, accomplishments, acts of service, good words, or a strong work ethic, we are ignoring God's unconditional gift of grace and subjecting others to the unrealistic standards and demands we have come to rely on; 2) Having a right view of ourselves is critical if we are to love and appreciate the value and worth others have as children of God; 3) Without a right view of ourselves, we can become judgmental, haughty, and unforgiving—quickly becoming closed off in our relationships, unable to love and serve others freely and without fear.
  - *Discuss*: Based on the demeaning way in which Isaac, Mary Katherine's father, treats other people, how do you think he views himself? Do you think he is able to accept God's unconditional love? Why or why not? In what ways do you struggle with accepting God's love? How do your relationships reflect this struggle? (Day 4)
  - *Read aloud*: Though fear and insecurity are marks of the human race, God gives us a higher calling. First Peter 2:9-10 reminds us:

    > *But you are a chosen race, a royal priesthood, a holy nation, a people for his own possession, that you may proclaim the excellencies of him who called you out of darkness into his marvelous light. Once you were not a people, but now you are God's people; once you had not received mercy, but now you have received mercy.* (ESV)

God has lavished mercy on us and has made us whole. Though our actions and our motivations will always be less than perfect, we are redeemed because of His great love for us. When we accept God's grace and redemption for

Notes

ourselves, embracing that good and perfect and undeserved gift, we have new eyes to see those around us. We see that they are less than perfect and that God has redeemed them. We see them as worthy, because that is how God sees them. We become more patient, loving, and willing to share of ourselves. We celebrate one another, despite our grand imperfections, because God has celebrated us.
- o *Discuss*: What do the following verses have to say about how we should relate to others? (Day 4)

> *But he gives us more grace. That is why Scripture says:*
>
> *"God opposes the proud*
> *but shows favor to the humble."*
> James 4:6

> *Accept one another, then, just as Christ accepted you, in order to bring praise to God.*
> Romans 15:7

> *Then Peter came to Jesus and asked, "Lord, how many times shall I forgive my brother or sister who sins against me? Up to seven times?"*
> Matthew 18:21

> *Live in harmony with one another. Do not be proud, but be willing to associate with people of low position. Do not be conceited.*
> Romans 12:16

> *Finally, all of you, be like-minded, be sympathetic, love one another, be compassionate and humble.*
> 1 Peter 3:8

- Explore how we all need the love and support of others in this life.
  - o Acknowledge that we all have insecurities and fears that plague our hearts, causing us to doubt ourselves and our abilities—sometimes to the point of stifling our hopes and dreams.
  - o *Read aloud*: Mary Katherine finds great support among the women in her life. Her grandmother, Leah, her cousins Naomi and Anna, and her friend Jamie all help Mary Katherine realize that her insecurities and doubts don't have to define her and that she can grow, flourish, and celebrate the ways in which she is gifted. Their loving, encouraging words help to combat the negative, wounding words that filled her childhood and call her to dream big. We

desperately need others in our lives to help us live in our strengths and combat our weaknesses. We need allies; we need family.

- o Compare the relationship that Mary Katherine has with her grandmother, Leah, to the relationship between Ruth and Naomi in the book of Ruth. Review the details of Naomi and Ruth's story in Day 5. Point out that Ruth trusted and loved Naomi enough to follow her to a strange land and a strange people, and Naomi loved Ruth enough to help her find a husband who would love and care for her. Like Ruth, Mary Katherine chose to follow her grandmother in her strong faith and gentle attitude, and like Naomi, Leah brought her granddaughter into her home to love and nurture her.
- o Have someone read aloud Ruth 1:16-17. *Discuss*: What do you imagine inspired Ruth to speak these strong, determined words? What must she have thought of Naomi and how Naomi treated her? How does Leah thoughtfully provide an environment for Mary Katherine in which she can flourish? How have you experienced this kind of mentorship or discipleship in your life? (Day 5) *Thoughts*: Leah allows Mary Katherine the freedom to practice her craft, and she encourages her in her pursuits. But above all, she reminds Mary Katherine that she is God's child and that nothing can change His love for her.

Notes

Week 4
The Reluctant Heart

Getting Started (10 minutes)

- Ask the group the following question:
  - What is the biggest decision you've ever had to make in your life? How did your decision change your life?
- Open with prayer, asking God to bless your time together.

A Few Minutes with Barbara (8-10 minutes)

Play the video for Week 4.

Let's Talk About It (10 minutes)

- Barbara shares why Mary Katherine has such a hard time deciding whether to join the Amish church and marry Jacob. Besides the lifelong implications of those decisions, there also is the issue of trust. How does trusting God help us in our decision making?
- According to Barbara, why do the Amish generally seem to struggle less with letting go and trusting God's will? How is letting go of our need to achieve perfection related to our ability to trust God?
- What insights does Barbara give us related to the importance of community to the Amish?
- What can we learn from the Amish about "living in the moment"? What are some things we can do to slow down and live in the moment each day?
- What other points or insights from the video would you like to discuss with the group?

Diving In (25 minutes)

Read Aloud

Decisions have a way of resting heavily on our shoulders. When it comes time to make the big calls, we are often reluctant—hesitant, frozen in indecision, fearful that we

Notes

Notes

will make the wrong choice, afraid that our heart and mind and logic will betray us and lead us down a path from which we will not recover.

Each and every day we are forced to make countless decisions. Some are small, and some are big. When it comes to making decisions, some of us are up to the task. We love taking decisive action and moving on, ready for the next step. We say, "Let's do it. Let's go for it!" Meanwhile, others of us are slow to decide, overly cautious, and wary of making decisions. Instead of committing, we tend to defer to other people, hoping that they will have more knowledge and courage to make the tough calls.

When it comes to making tough decisions in our lives, it's natural for us to feel afraid. It's normal to be reluctant when making big commitments. It's common to feel that we must make the *right* decision, and that making the wrong one will cause our lives to spin recklessly out of control or lead us down paths we don't want.

Laboring over making a tough decision can break us down and make us weary and confused. Like Mary Katherine, we can worry that maybe we've missed God's will for our lives or misinterpreted what He's trying to tell us. We can reach a place where we become insecure and doubtful, wondering if God is silent—or worse, absent.

Discuss

- Different personalities react differently when called upon to make decisions. Which camp do you tend to fit in? Do you make decisions easily, or are you slow to commit? Why do you think you react the way you do? (Day 1)
- Mary Katherine struggles with decisions about her future, including whether to join the Amish church and to have a relationship with Jacob. Have you ever struggled with a big decision and felt unsure about what God wanted you to do? What was the situation?
- To what extent do you think God should factor into your decision making? To what extent does He actually factor into how you make decisions? (Day 1)

Read Aloud

Do you believe God belongs in your decision making? It's an interesting question to ask because most of us Christians would say, "Yes, of course God belongs in our decision making." But to what extent do we really believe that to be true? Some people seem to believe that God should weigh in a yes or no on every little decision in their lives; others feel that, if we are believers in the work Jesus did for us on the cross and have the Holy Spirit inside of us, God already exists in everything that we do and every decision that we make. Perhaps the better question is, if you are a Christian, why *wouldn't* God factor into your decision making?

Discuss

- Read aloud Acts 17:24-28, having a different group member read each verse. Then ask, "What does each verse have to say about God's authority and power in each of our lives?" (Day 1)
  Thoughts:
  Verse 24: *God made the whole world and everything in it; He did not need humans to help create it.*
  Verse 25: *God doesn't need anything from us; He is sufficient in and of Himself and gives life to all of us.*
  Verse 26: *God created everything and knows about all of our days.*
  Verse 27: *God is near; He wants us to reach out to Him and to come to Him for fulfillment and guidance.*
  Verse 28: *We exist because of Him; we were created in His image (Genesis 1) and are called His children (1 John 3:1).*
- After reading and studying this passage, what do you think is the correct posture we should have before God—fear, humility, or insecurity? (Hint: check out 2 Chronicles 7:14.)

Notes

Read Aloud

In the book of John, we read about an event that happened on Passover, a night when Israel celebrated God's provision for His people. Jesus and His disciples sat at a dimly lit table. The mood was somber. Jesus had just revealed to them that He would be leaving them, that His time on Earth was short-lived. Sad and confused, the disciples wondered what they would do when Jesus left. Where would they go? How would they carry on?

Certainly Jesus spoke gently, softly: "Do not let your hearts be troubled....I will not leave you as orphans; I will come to you" (John 14:1a, 18). Though the disciples had been in the actual presence of God in the form of His Son, Jesus, they came unhinged as uncertainties about their futures and their ministry began to overwhelm them. Though they had seen Jesus perform miracles with their own eyes and experienced His gentle leading, they still had a hard time wrapping their minds around what it takes to truly follow Jesus: trust.

Jesus told the disciples that, though He was leaving them in body, He was not leaving them alone: "But the Advocate, the Holy Spirit, whom the Father will send in my name, will teach you all things and will remind you of everything I have said to you" (John 14:26). And the same is true for us. Though we have never felt Jesus' physical touch or heard Him speak to the restless crowds, He is with us nonetheless, and we can trust that the Holy Spirit leads us and directs our steps. Though we may never fully understand His ways, we can choose to trust in His Word and His love for us, and we can choose to obey.

In order to make the best decision for our lives, we must choose to trust that God's ways are higher than ours and that only He can make the impossible perfect.

Notes

Discuss

- Do you find it hard to trust God at times? In what ways? (Day 2)
- Jesus said, "Peace I leave with you; my peace I give you. I do not give to you as the world gives" (John 14:27a). What promises of peace does this world offer us, and how is God's peace different? (Day 2)
  Thoughts: The promises of peace and protection that we establish for ourselves are often shallow—we buy insurance, we strive to leave a legacy for ourselves, and we put up walls around our hearts to keep out hurt. God's peace is vastly deeper; He promises to be with us and never to leave us. He is our sufficiency, and He will never fail us.
- Have you ever taken a leap of faith and followed God's leading, even though you were unsure about how things would turn out? What happened? (Day 2)

Read Aloud

For many of us, trusting God with our hearts is the easy part—it's what comes after that seems so complicated. Our minds are flooded with questions: Which church should I join? Where does God want me to serve? What should I change about my life? Am I serving Him in the "right" way? Does God want me to sell everything I have and move to Africa? Sometimes we get so caught up in trying to serve God in the *right* ways that we tend to miss the big picture.

Micah 6:8 says, "He has shown you, O man, what *is* good; and what does the LORD require of you but to do justly, to love mercy, and to walk humbly with your God?" (NKJV). God doesn't ask us to try harder or work harder in order to win His approval and love. He says the terms are already worked out: to love and care for others and to walk in intimate relationship with Him. All the other details will sort themselves out, and He will make our paths clear, including those places where He wants us to serve, using our God-given gifts and talents.

Discuss

- Mary Katherine struggles with her decision to join the Amish church. Have you ever struggled with the decision to join a church? If so, what made that decision difficult for you? How did God lead you through that process?
- The total commitment of the Amish to their way of life and to their faith cannot be denied. In every aspect of their lives, seven days a week, they are committed to living out the things they believe to be true, especially when it comes to living in community with other believers. Do you find it hard to commit to and live whole-heartedly in your community (in whatever form that community takes—church, school, neighborhood, friendships)?

Read Aloud

Growing in intimacy with others demands a lot of us; it means that we must be willing to risk being vulnerable and authentic. It demands that we put aside our reluctance and fear and believe that, as children of God who are *already* fully loved and accepted by our heavenly Father, we can be exactly whom He has created us to be. We don't have to hide in the shadows of our imperfections and shortcomings, but we can step into the light of His grace to fully love and accept others and be the community of believers God calls us to be. We don't have to put the pressure on our communities to define us, because we have already been defined by our state as forgiven, loved children of God.

This knowledge frees us to love others and serve where God leads us, without fear or regret, knowing that our lives are in His hands. The pressure to make all the *right* decisions is off!

Discuss

Notes

- Have someone read aloud Hebrews 10:19-25. Then ask, "How does what Jesus has already done for you allow you to live within the community of believers? How can this knowledge change your perspective on church/community?" (Day 3)
  Thoughts: Jesus has already freed us from our sin and given us life; therefore, He has freed us to live fully in whom He made each of us to be. We can claim His goodness, His love, and His grace in every situation and every relationship, and we can be united with other believers in those truths. We don't have to give in to fear, insecurity, and reluctance; instead, we can fully serve those around us, knowing how much we are loved and cared for by our Creator.

In Closing (5 minutes)

Close your time together in prayer, acknowledging that God is trustworthy and sufficient to meet all our needs. Pray that we would learn to rest in that knowledge and trust in His goodness and provision. Acknowledge that He is big enough to handle any decisions that we face, and because He is with us, we can be confident and not reluctant. Pray that we would commit fully to the communities that we are placed in, and that we can give fully of ourselves to these communities because of God's great love for us.

If You Have More Time
(30 additional minutes; use before In Closing)

Choose from the following:
- Discuss how we spend our time, energy, and resources.
  - *Read aloud*: Most of us lead very busy lives. But instead of reluctantly doing

Notes

everything we *think* we should be doing every day, what if we have the courage to step back and say, Wait a minute—is this the *right* thing? Believe it or not, God cares about how we spend our time, energy, and resources. Consider Jesus' encounter with Mary and Martha in Luke 10.

- o Have someone read aloud Luke 10:38-42.
- o *Read aloud*: In this story, we see Martha in the kitchen, frantically trying to prepare for her guests. Who could blame her? It was a *big* deal to have Jesus show up at your house. Any of us would have done the same. So when Martha got frustrated and flustered, Jesus spoke to her kindly. "Martha, it's okay. Stop for a minute. Come and sit with me." Martha wasn't doing anything bad; in fact, she was probably playing into her natural strengths of organization and hosting. And Jesus wasn't chastising or patronizing her; He just wanted her to know that she didn't have to find her identity in being the best cook, hostess, or housekeeper in the village. Jesus just wanted her to know that she was enough in His presence, and that she could set aside her work and rest in that knowledge.
- o *Discuss*: In what areas of your life are you spending your time and your energy because you think those things define who you are and give you worth? After reading Martha's story, what do you hear God saying to you about those things? (Day 4)

• Talk about what it means to live wholeheartedly.
- o *Read aloud*: In our quest to live the lives that God intends for us, we often come to a place where we are not sure what to do. There is a fork in the road, or a fallen tree blocks the path, or the path disappears into the woods altogether. Without any pointing arrows or "Go This Way" signs, we're left without directions about what to do. We become confused and frustrated. We overthink the solutions. We wonder, Should it be this hard? Why isn't it clear which way I should go? Am I doing something wrong? Suddenly the clear, easy path turns treacherous. We start to be afraid of what we can't see, of what might be lurking out there. We wonder if God is present and why He didn't equip us better for the journey if He wanted us to walk this path. We must let go of our idea of perfection and learn to trust in God's will for us. We must make the tough decisions that require us to give something up in order to get something else; we must learn that what is perfect is exactly what God has for us. Though we know our lives will never be perfect, that knowledge certainly doesn't stop us from trying, does it? Whether it's getting more "stuff" or working hard to get that dream job or having some unrealistic expectations of those around us, it seems we're always thinking that the "grass is greener on the other side" and striving to get there. But when this becomes our way of living, we become broken and distracted, our hearts divided between letting God be God and taking control of our own lives again and again. Learning to live wholeheartedly requires us to learn to trust God and to receive His love. It requires that we are committed to following God's leading and that we are willing to step out in trust and obedience when He calls us.

o *Discuss*: Have you experienced a time when your perfect ideal of something was shattered? What happened, and how did you respond? Did that affect your view of God? If so, how? (Day 5)
o Have someone read aloud the following verses: Matthew 22:37, Ephesians 6:7, Colossians 3:17. What does each verse have to say about living wholeheartedly? (Day 5)

Thoughts: Matthew 22:37: Love God with every part of you. Ephesians 6:7: Serve wholeheartedly. Colossians 3:17: Everything you do, do it for God.

Notes

Week 5
The Romantic Heart

Getting Started (10 minutes)

- Ask the group one of the following questions:
  - As a child, what was your favorite fairy tale? What did you love most about it?
  - Who is your favorite literary or movie heroine? Why do you like her? What about her story appeals to you?
- Open with prayer, asking God to bless your time together.

A Few Minutes with Barbara (8-10 minutes)
Play the video for Week 5.

Let's Talk About It (10 minutes)

- What does Barbara tell us about the Amish view of love? What does she suggest is required for a thriving marriage? Would you add anything to the list?
- Barbara discusses how Mary Katherine's past hurts and self-esteem affect her ability to love Jacob. What insights does she share related to what helps Mary Katherine to open herself up to Jacob and embrace her feelings for him?
- What does Barbara say about how God's love frees us to love others?
- Barbara closes by acknowledging that most of us dream about a fairy tale romance from the time we are little girls, and we're disappointed when real life doesn't measure up. What is the true romance intended to satisfy this desire of our hearts?
- What other points or insights from the video would you like to discuss with the group?

Diving In (25 minutes)

Read Aloud

Read aloud the following excerpt from chapter 18 of *Her Restless Heart*.

Jamie smirked. "C'mon, everyone, grab a plate and let's eat."…
Each of [the girls] took a plate piled with several slices of pizza and a can of soda

Notes

into the living room. Anna won the right to choose the movie—a DVD of Tangled—*and soon Rapunzel was letting down her hair, song filled the apartment, and everyone became absorbed in the story.*

Mary Katherine was reminded of that night in the pizza place when she'd dressed in Englisch *clothes and left her hair loose—no tightly drawn bun, no pristine* kapp. *Jacob had seemed to be fascinated by her hair, staring at it.*

The fairy tale played on. The one on the television screen, that is. She wasn't so sheltered in her community that she didn't know about fairy tales. She'd read a number of them in books that she'd checked out from the library bookmobile. Maybe she'd even had a few girlish dreams of a handsome man falling in love with her.

But in the end, she was too practical to really believe in them. She didn't understand the Englisch *fascination with such. Wasn't it better to look at love the way the Plain people did? You didn't wait for some handsome stranger—you dated the boy you'd grown up seeing in church, in* schul, *at singings and other social events. You knew you'd be his partner in his life's work—and he in yours if you chose to work as well as raise your* kinner—*so you made certain that your love ran true and deep and it wasn't just some story you'd made up about him.*

Discuss

- Why do you think women love a good fairy tale? Have you ever had your own fairy-tale experience? What happened and how did it make you feel? (Day 1)
- How do you feel about the Amish view of love relationships? Do you tend to lean more toward the practical side of love or the more romantic side? (Day 1)

Read Aloud

We all long to experience the adventure, elation, and perfect resolution of the fairy tale, and we're often disappointed when life doesn't measure up. So how do we cope when everyday life throws cold water on the fire of our relationships? When who we thought was Mr. Right doesn't call after the second date? When the unbridled romance we were expecting is something more like lukewarm companionship? When our deep desire to love and be loved is harder than we expected? We turn our eyes toward the One who loves us beyond what we could ever hope for.

In Jeremiah 31:3, the Lord says, "I have loved you with an everlasting love." In his letter to the Ephesians, Paul prays that his fellow Christians "will have power, together with all the Lord's holy people, to grasp how wide and long and high and deep is the love of Christ, and to know this love that surpasses knowledge—that you may be filled to the measure of all the fullness of God" (3:18-19). Talk about a dramatic kind of love!

Have you ever considered that you are already in a grand love story, written before the beginning of time? In this love story, a white knight—a Savior—has come and rescued you so that you might have the love that you've always dreamed of. He calls you Beloved, and He gave up everything so that you could stand at His side.

In Christ, we have the ultimate "fairy tale," and no other relationship on Earth can replace the perfect one that He offers. Ephesians 2:4-5 says, "But God, being rich in mercy, because of the great love with which he loved us, even when we were dead in our trespasses, made us alive together with Christ—by grace you have been saved" (ESV).

Discuss

- How does knowing that you are completely and unconditionally loved by God free you to experience healthy love relationships with others? (Day 1)
  Thoughts: When we accept God's unconditional love for us and find our acceptance in Him, we can release the heavy burden we put on our love relationships to provide the love and acceptance we need. We then can enjoy others for who they are instead of asking them to carry the weight of our identity.

Notes

Read Aloud

From the very beginning, we women were created for companionship. We were made with a great capacity to love and a great desire to be loved in return. Whether married or single, we all have this need for love and companionship. And though God is and should be our number-one source for fulfillment, the desire to walk through life together with another is a God-given desire that was meant for our good. After God created Adam, He said, "It's not good for the Man to be alone" (Genesis 2:18 *THE MESSAGE*). He wanted Adam to have someone to share his life with, someone whom he could hold and talk to and laugh with. Adam needed Eve, and she needed him.

Discuss

- Even though the desire for intimate companionship—the desire to walk through life with another—is given to us by God, have you ever struggled with this desire, feeling that it is somehow less than spiritual? Why or why not? (Day 2)

Read Aloud

Marriage didn't just happen; God created it. After Eve was created, Adam said, "This is now bone of my bones and flesh of my flesh.... That is why a man leaves his father and mother and is united to his wife, and they become one flesh" (Genesis 2:23-24). God conceived of and ordained marriage, and therefore it is good.

Apart from our relationship with God, marriage is most likely the deepest and most intimate relationship we can experience here on Earth. It is a wonderful thing to be able to walk through life's ups and downs with another person, although fallible, and to experience the love of God through someone else's love and care. But in order for a marriage relationship to thrive, it must be put into proper perspective as secondary to your relationship with God.

Her Restless Heart

Notes

In addition to having the proper perspective, a thriving marriage also requires hard work. Relationships are hard. And in order to be able to love someone else well, we first need to know and be filled with the love of God. First John 4:19 says, "We love because he first loved us" (ESV). God wants us to learn to love each other well.

Discuss

- Why do you think God created marriage? (Day 2)
- Based on your own life experiences, what is your view of marriage? Do you see it as a good thing, something to desire and celebrate, or do you have a doubting or cynical view of marriage? Explain your response. (Day 2)
- Leah tells Mary Katherine that there was a reason we weren't put on Earth by ourselves: we're supposed to learn something from other people, and they from us. What is something you think God wants us to learn from one another through marriage? (Day 2)
- Do you struggle with keeping your marriage (or significant relationships) in proper perspective relative to your relationship with God? If so, in what ways? (Day 2)

Read Aloud

Our culture sends us all kinds of mixed messages about what an ideal dating relationship and an ideal marriage should look like, including the roles of husbands and wives. In the world's perspective, the good of the individual is often valued above the partnership, encouraging a battle of the sexes that rarely finds a favorable conclusion.

Too often, it seems that women today are caught in the middle of this battle, struggling to understand what it means to have a good marriage. There is a lot of confusion and emotion surrounding the roles of husbands and wives, and more and more, marriages are suffering because of it. Women want to be good wives to their husbands and to be valued and fulfilled as women. But they don't always know how to make both happen.

Discuss

- What would you say are the messages and/or expectations in our culture today regarding the roles of husbands and wives, and what it takes to make a marriage good? (Day 4)
- Based on what you know about the Amish, what are their traditional beliefs about marriage and the roles of husband and wife? (If you are reading the novel, which characters give us insight into these beliefs—and how?) (Day 4)

Read Aloud

There are (and always will be) countless perspectives vying for a voice on this issue, but we should be concerned with only one: God's. What does God say about marriage and the roles of husbands and wives?

- Have someone read aloud Ephesians 5:21-33.

Two key words in this passage are *love* and *respect*. Although throughout the ages many people have used the "wives submit to your husbands" command to demean and subdue, it is clear that this is *not* what God intends in these verses! God does not intend for women to be lesser partners or to be treated in a demeaning or dismissive way. As a matter of fact, husbands are instructed to love—cherish—their wives as Christ loved the church. And how did Christ do that? He gave up everything—His own safety, comfort, and even His life—in order to restore the church (His bride) to the full, rich life that was meant for her.

Discuss

Note: This issue may be a touchy one for some, so be sensitive to this emotionally charged topic. Continually point your group back to God's command to "submit to one another out of reverence for Christ" (Ephesians 5:21). Emphasize that although these verses from Ephesians 5 have been used recklessly by some, it is not God's intention that anyone be demeaned or subdued by these words. It's also important to note that abuse of any kind—verbal, emotional, or physical—is never acceptable in God's sight, and it is certainly not supported by this Scripture, or any other in the Bible. Abusive behavior of a spouse should never be overlooked in the name of "respect."

- What is your initial response or reaction to this oft-quoted passage in Ephesians? What emotions does it stir in you? (Day 4)
- Paul begins this important passage in Ephesians by saying, "Submit to one another out of reverence for Christ" (v. 21). What does it mean to submit to one another, and why are we to do it "out of reverence for Christ"? (Day 4)
  Thoughts: Submitting to one another is showing love and respect to one another; we do it because Christ commands it, and we desire to obey His commands because we love Him. Sometimes this means actively choosing to love not because we particularly feel like it, but because Christ commands it.
- If you are reading the novel, how does Jacob model for Mary Katherine that he has a correct biblical view of what a husband should be? (Day 4)
  Thoughts: He is kind and sensitive, and he supports Mary Katherine in her craft. He doesn't want to subdue her spirit or "rein her in" but desires a true companion in life.

In Closing (5 minutes)

Close the session in prayer, thanking the Lord for the desire He has given us to love and connect with others. Pray that He would help you to know that this desire for

Notes

relationship with others is good while remembering that He wants you to desire Him above all else. Thank Him for the ways in which He so faithfully and tenderly cares for you.

If You Have More Time
(30 additional minutes; use before In Closing)

Choose from the following:
- Talk about how God is able to heal the hurts from our pasts so that we can move forward in our relationships.
    - *Read aloud*: In the novel, Mary Katherine becomes very upset when Jacob accuses her of seeing another man, Daniel, behind his back. Mary Katherine is confused and upset by his accusations; she is hurt that he would think such things about her. In her pain, she is reminded of how her father has hurt her in the past, and she finds it hard to forgive Jacob, wondering if he, like her father, will continue to break her faith and trust. Though our hearts may be wounded and bruised, God is our Healer, and He is able to lift the hurt and pain of our pasts from our shoulders and bear it on His own. He gives us new life and hope and allows us to start fresh, supported by His great love for us. When it comes to our relationships, we must turn over our past hurts to God and allow Him to heal us and quiet our fears so that we can confidently move forward in the relationships He has given us. We must trust that God is the One Who heals our hearts so that we are free to love others fully—without fear.
    - *Discuss*: What does James 1:17 say about God's nature, and what assurance does that give you? What might this assurance mean for your relationships? (Day 3) *Thoughts*: God is the giver of all good gifts, and His nature does not change. Therefore we can trust what He says and know that He is determined to give us good things.
- Explore the importance of accepting the gifts of others in our lives—especially our spouses.
    - *Read aloud*: Like much of the Amish community, Mary Katherine's parents were farmers, and being the only child, she was required to work on the farm alongside them. She disliked the tasks she had to do on the farm and resented her father's penchant for assigning her the most distasteful chores. As a result, she came to hate farming and was all too happy to escape to the safety of her grandmother's shop. But Jacob loves farming, and he hopes that one day Mary Katherine will come to love and appreciate it as much as he does. For a husband and wife to have a relationship that is rich and vibrant, each must learn to embrace what the other loves. They must celebrate each other's strengths and learn how those strengths can complement the strengths of the other, making the relationship stronger. As we discussed in Week 3, God has made each of us

with intention and love, giving each of us specific gifts and strengths that make us unique. When we are able to rest in the gifts God has given us, knowing that God created each of us uniquely and that we have a role to fill in the world, we can accept the gifts of others in our lives. We don't have to compete or one-up each other, quarrelling about whose gift is better or more useful; instead, we can celebrate, embrace, and appreciate the richness that others bring into our lives.

o *Discuss*: If you are married, how alike are you and your spouse? What are your differences? If you are not married, how alike and different are or were your parents? Have those differences been a struggle in your marriage—or your parents' marriage? If so, how? How are you learning—or how did your parents learn—to embrace those differences to make a stronger marriage? (Day 5)

o Invite participants to imagine what might happen in Mary Katherine and Jacob's relationship once they marry. *Discuss*: What do you think their relationship and life together will look like? (Day 5)

Notes

Week 6
The Satisfied Heart

Getting Started (10 minutes)

- Ask the group the following questions:
  - What makes you angry—livid even? In what instances do you tend to get defensive? What makes you want to break all your dishes or really tell someone what you think of his or her actions? What makes you sad? When do you tend to be sensitive?
- Open with prayer, asking God to bless your time together.

A Few Minutes with Barbara (8-10 minutes)

Play the video for Week 6.

Let's Talk About It (10 minutes)

- Barbara talks about how we see God at work in Mary Katherine's life throughout the novel. What are some of the things she highlights? Looking back on your own life, what are some of the evidences that God has always been at work?
- According to Barbara, what encourages Mary Katherine to pursue reconciliation with her parents? Is there a person or persons in your life you need to pursue reconciliation with? How does Mary Katherine's story encourage you?
- What does Barbara say we can be sure of in the midst of pain? Do her observations resonate with you? Why or why not?
- Barbara talks about a time when she had to trust that God was working a difficult situation for her good. What can help us to keep on trusting God during times when we cannot see what God is doing?
- Barbara shares what she learned from writing the novel. What have you learned from participating in this study?
- What other points or insights from the video would you like to discuss with the group?

Notes

Notes

Diving In (25 minutes)

Read Aloud

Though the paths that our lives take often lead us through ups and downs, joys and sorrows, the Lord is continually renewing us and drawing us closer to Him. This week we've explored how putting our hope, trust, and faith in God allows us to live fully and freely, enabling us to take each step as it comes, confident in His love for us and in the assurance that He will never leave or forsake us. This hope gives us a boldness to step out in faith and follow where God leads—our hearts fully satisfied in Him.

A few minutes ago, we shared some things that really get our emotions going. But maybe you struggle with emotions, thinking that Christians aren't really supposed to feel any of these strong emotions. We Christians are supposed to walk around in a happy stupor, never feeling angry or frustrated or disgusted. That's what a Christian is really supposed to be like, right?

Often we feel like a "less-than" Christian when we're overwhelmed by our emotions. But hear this: emotions are not bad things! God created human beings in His own image, and Scripture talks about God having a range of emotions—happy, sad, angry, compassionate, and so forth.

Emotions are not the enemy. It's natural for us to *feel* things—and we can cycle through many emotions on any given day. But these emotions must not control us or define us; instead, we should examine our emotions as clues about what is going on in our hearts and see them as signposts to show us where God is working in our lives—where He wants us to pay attention.

When we stop to consider the feelings of restlessness and frustration that often consume us, we generally find that we feel this way because we are looking for satisfaction in things that ultimately can't satisfy us. Our minds may be easily fooled into thinking that we can find fulfillment and satisfaction from the things of this world, but deep down in our hearts we know the truth: the only thing that can fulfill us is the love of God.

In Psalm 63, we find King David hiding out in the desert, on the run from his enemies who are pursuing him with deadly intent.

- Have someone read aloud Psalm 63:1-5.

David has known the goodness of God in his success as king, and he has experienced God's provision, presence, love, and favor. Now, in dire straits and facing an uncertain future, it would be tempting for David to feel abandoned by God, to feel frustrated because he is in such a precarious situation. But David knows the only thing that can sustain his hope is the Lord.

In the desert of his circumstances, David knows that God will provide for him. Not only does he know that God will provide, he also proclaims that God's provision and love defy every expectation he can imagine.

God's love for us, expressed in His work on our behalf through the cross, goes far, far beyond any hope or expectation of love and acceptance we could ever imagine. God pursues our hearts with a relentless love; we are more loved and accepted than we could ever comprehend. He delights in us and is pleased to give us every good thing.

Though Mary Katherine looks to her family and her community for approval, those paths simply seem to fuel her frustration and her restlessness. Even her weaving—the craft that she loves and finds success in—contributes to her feeling that she doesn't fit well into her farm-centric community. But once she realizes that God loves her and cares for her and has a plan for her life, she is able to rest in her identity as His child first and foremost. Then she is able to make the big decisions she is facing in life.

Notes

Discuss

- During your time in this study, how have you felt God saying to you, "Put down your hope in [this thing or person] and find your satisfaction in me"? (Day 1)
- What emotion(s) are driving you these days? How might the Lord be calling to you through these emotions? (Day 1)

Read Aloud

When our hearts are able to find peace and satisfaction in God, we are free to be our true selves and live fully in our giftedness. Like Mary Katherine, many of us struggle in life, wondering where we belong. When things don't go perfectly or smoothly, we tend to question ourselves and lose confidence in our abilities.

Though Mary Katherine likes to push the limits of her creativity in her craft by experimenting with new patterns, techniques, and color combinations, she is daunted by the opportunity to speak to a college class about it. Having never set foot on a college campus, she feels unworthy and even a bit embarrassed to think the students will want to hear anything she has to say. But she pushes herself to speak to the class, and it goes great, giving Mary Katherine the confidence she needs to keep working, celebrating her gifts, and finding joy in something that God has gifted her to do.

God delights in the fact that we are all gifted in different ways. He specifically created each of us with different gifts and strengths. If you have children, think about the different gifts and personalities within your family. You would probably acknowledge that, although they may sometimes present challenges and disagreements, the differences that exist between the members make the family stronger, more interesting, and richer. Considering that God has created each of us, it's clear that He feels the same way about us.

Though we can't pick and choose the natural gifts and abilities of our own children, God *can* and *did* choose yours specifically to be used by you.

Notes

- Have someone read aloud Psalm 139: 1-3, 13-16.

The same passage in (*THE MESSAGE*) Bible reads:

> *Oh yes, you shaped me first inside, then out;*
> *   you formed me in my mother's womb.*
> *I thank you, High God—you're breathtaking!*
> *   Body and soul, I am marvelously made!*
> *   I worship in adoration—what a creation!*
> *You know me inside and out,*
> *   you know every bone in my body;*
> *You know exactly how I was made, bit by bit,*
> *   how I was sculpted from nothing into something.*
> *Like an open book, you watched me grow from conception to birth;*
> *   all the stages of my life were spread out before you,*
> *The days of my life all prepared*
> *   before I'd even lived one day.*
>
> (vv. 13-16)

God wants us to grow in our talents and to be confident of how much He loves us. He wants us to blossom. If we as parents are devoted to fostering and nurturing the talents, abilities, and strengths of our own children, how much more God wants to do that for us! No matter how much we may feel that we don't measure up to some perceived notion of greatness, God regards us as fully approved and accepted. That knowledge should make us rejoice! As such, we are free to try, fail, try again, succeed, and enjoy the process.

Discuss

- Over the course of this study, have you felt God speaking to you about the unique ways in which He has gifted you? In what ways do you feel God is challenging and encouraging you to "push your own limits" and explore those gifts further?
- What are some things that might hold you back from exploring and growing in your gifts? How can you give those fears and obstacles to God, asking for His help and guidance?
  Thoughts: Some examples might be family obligations or time constraints or just plain fear.
- Read aloud Colossians 3:23-24 and 1 Corinthians 10:31; discuss what these verses say about God's plan for our gifts.
  Thoughts: Do everything as if working solely for the Lord—do it for His glory.

Read Aloud

Throughout this study, we have learned about our deep need for love and acceptance, and about how God is able to meet every desire of our hearts. As we see in Mary Katherine's story, when we are able to lay down the fears that hold us hostage and the doubts that so easily hold us back, we will see that God is at work in our lives, actively engaged and laying out a path for us that leads us to walk in closer communion with Him.

When we are secure in the knowledge that we are fully loved and accepted, we can begin to walk that path in freedom, constantly surprised by God's unexpected but wonderful gifts. As God begins to open Mary Katherine's heart and calm her fears, she discovers wonderful surprises that God has in store for her—the love of a wonderful man and fulfilling work.

Mary Katherine's journey isn't easy or predictable, but her struggles prove necessary and worthy because they lead her closer to the heart of God. There she can rest and be renewed by His love and affection, free of binding fear and nagging doubt.

Our Father, the Great Restorer, makes all things new in His time. We need only listen and respond. Hear these words from Romans 12:1-2:

Notes

> *Take your everyday, ordinary life—your sleeping, eating, going-to-work, and walking-around life—and place it before God as an offering. Embracing what God does for you is the best thing you can do for him. Don't become so well-adjusted to your culture that you fit into it without even thinking. Instead, fix your attention on God. You'll be changed from the inside out. Readily recognize what he wants from you, and quickly respond to it. Unlike the culture around you, always dragging you down to its level of immaturity, God brings the best out of you, develops well-formed maturity in you.*
>
> *(THE MESSAGE)*

Discuss

- Have you ever been surprised by God? How? What happened? (Day 5)
- Over the course of this study, in what ways is God leading you to be bold and courageous, trusting that He has everything under control and is working it for good? (Day 5)
- What have you learned through this study about trusting in God and resting in His love for you? (Day 5)

In Closing (5 minutes)

Revelation 21:5 proclaims: "He who was seated on the throne said, 'I am making everything new!' Then he said, 'Write this down, for these words are trustworthy and true.'" Take a few minutes in quiet reflection to review the words you wrote in your

Notes

workbook that God has been speaking to you through your time in this study of His Word (see Day 5). Invite the women to share their thoughts with one another as they are willing.

Close the session with a time of prayer, thanking God for His goodness and faithfulness. Ask Him for the boldness, strength, and confidence to trust Him with every aspect of your lives, and for the ability to run to Him when the doubts and fears of life are too much. Pray that all of you would be able to live fully and freely in Him from this day forward.

If You Have More Time
(30 additional minutes; use before In Closing)

Choose one of the following:
- Talk about the areas in our lives where we need reconciliation.
  - *Read aloud:* Throughout Scripture, we read beautiful words about God's desire for peace, reconciliation, and healing for His children. As Jesus walked the Earth and ministered to the people around Him, His heart for mercy, healing, and transformation was evident in His every action. The New Testament is full of stories of Jesus' interactions with people who were hurting and in need. (If you want to read some of these, see John 8:1-22 for the woman caught in adultery, Matthew 9:18-22 for the woman who touched Jesus' robe, and John 5:1-15 for the man at the pool in Bethesda.) These encounters with Jesus show that God is our great Healer. Just as He heals our bodies, so He longs to heal our hearts and our relationships. With His presence and guidance, broken relationships can be repaired, and past hurts can be healed.
  - Talk about how we see God working in the hearts of Mary Katherine and her parents in *Her Restless Heart*. Note that as the novel progresses, Mary Katherine finds she is more and more open to having a restored relationship with her parents. Though she is sifting through years of hurt and pain, Mary Katherine begins to see the hope that God can and will restore their relationship.
  - *Discuss:* During this study, has God revealed to you any areas in your life that need reconciliation? If so, how is He leading you to pursue peace in those areas? (Day 2) *Note: You might consider breaking into pairs or small groups for this discussion.*
- Explore the benefits of truly living in community.
  - *Read aloud:* There is no denying the wisdom, support, and love that being in community with other believers brings into our lives. Truly living in community—having faith in others and opening ourselves up to them freely and authentically—enriches our lives and challenges us to grow in our faith and blossom as part of the family of God.
  - Have someone read aloud Matthew 18:20. Then discuss how community played a role in Mary Katherine's decision to join the church and stay in the community.

Thoughts: Leah—probably along with her friends—likely had been praying for Mary Katherine. Mary Katherine realized all the love and support that she had in her community, which made her want to remain there with them. Having such a solid, loving group of people around her—her grandmother, Leah; cousins Naomi and Anna; Jacob; and even her *Englisch* friend, Jamie—gave Mary Katherine the reassurance that she could be whom God uniquely made her to be, and that her community would support her as she pursued her dreams.

o *Discuss*: How does Mary Katherine's story encourage you to live fully in *your* community—to both give and receive love and support? (Day 4)

Notes

Notes

Week 1

1. Matthew Henry, "Psalm 46," in *Matthew Henry Commentary on the Whole Bible* (1706; BibleStudyTools.com, 2012), http://www.biblestudytools.com/commentaries/matthew-henry-complete/psalms/46.html

2. St. Augustine, *The Confessions of St. Augustine, Bishop of Hippo* (398; Cyber Library, 2002), bk. I, chap. I, http://www.leaderu.com/cyber/books/augconfessions/bk1.html

Week 2

1. William Faulkner, *Requiem for a Nun* (1951), Act I, scene iii.

Week 3

1. Macrina Wiederkehr, quoted in M. S. Ryan, ed., *A Grateful Heart* (New York: Fine Communications), 71.

God Wants to Rewrite Your Story

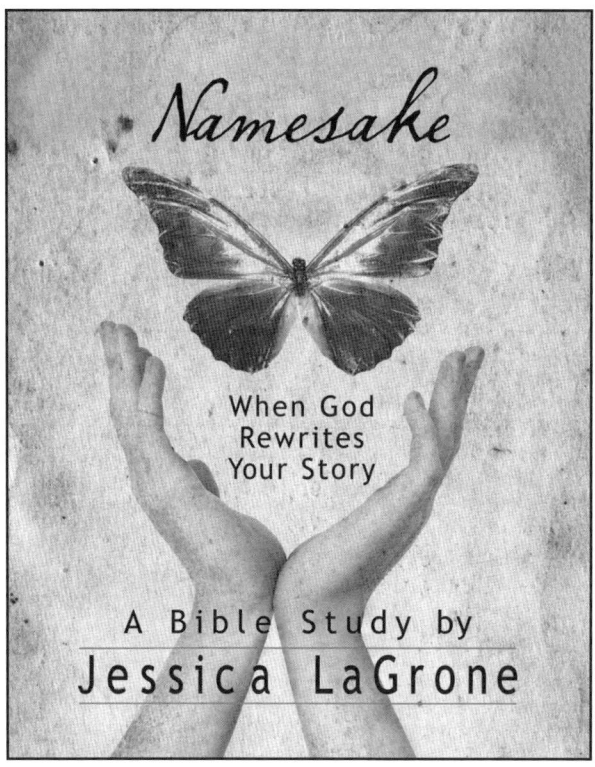

Meet popular author, speaker, blogger, and pastor Jessica LaGrone—a dynamic, new voice in in-depth Bible study. In her six-week Bible study, Namesake, she explores the power of God to transform our lives and destinies by focusing on six biblical stories about persons who encountered God and whose names and lives were forever changed. As you meet Abraham, Sarah, Jacob, Naomi, Daniel, Peter, and an unnamed woman, you will discover that God wants to be just as intimately involved in your own story, offering an identity that shines with the purpose for which you were created—to know Him through His Son, Jesus, and to become more and more like Him, bringing God glory for His name's sake.

Participant Book • Leader Guide • DVD • Mini Preview Book
Leader Kit (includes one of each component)

Jessica LaGrone is Pastor of Worship at The Woodlands United Methodist Church in The Woodlands, Texas. An acclaimed preacher, teacher, and writer— including her popular blog "Reverend Mother" (jessicalagrone.com)—she enjoys speaking at retreats and events at churches throughout the United States. She and her husband, Jim, have two young children, Drew and Kate.

For more information, visit AbingdonPress.com, AbingdonWomen.com,
or your favorite Christian retailer.

Another Great Bible Study from the Faith and Fiction Series

Popular Christian fiction author Melody Carlson draws upon her novels in the Inn at Shining Waters trilogy to invite women on an exciting journey toward healing. Using the stories, themes, and characters of the novels as a backdrop—much in the way that Jesus used stories to teach important truths and principles—this 8-week, DVD-based study explores the need for forgiveness and mercy in our lives and the role that second chances and new beginnings play in healing our spirits and our relationships. *Abingdon Press.*

Participant Book • Leader Guide • DVD

Melody Carlson is the award-winning author of more than two hundred books and the recipient of a Romantic Times Career Achievement Award and a Rita Award. She and her husband live in Central Oregon.

For more information, visit AbingdonPress.com, AbingdonWomen.com, or your favorite Christian retailer.

Be Transformed by God's Love and Acceptance

Every woman longs to know that she is loved, accepted, and valued. Yet, many wonder, "Does God really love me as I am? Do I really matter to God?" In this 8-week Bible study, award-winning gospel singer, songwriter, and teacher Babbie Mason helps women of all ages and walks of life to discover the depth and breadth of God's great love and acceptance. Drawing upon her own personal journey to understand how much God loves her—not as a singer or teacher but as God's beloved daughter—she equips women to accept God's unfailing love as they understand and claim seven biblical promises.

Participant Book • Leader Guide • DVD • Mini Preview Book
Leader Kit (includes one of each component plus a bonus music CD)

Babbie Mason is a Dove Award-winning, Grammy-nominated, American Gospel singer and songwriter; a tireless women's conference speaker; a worship leader through her Embrace: A Worship Celebration for Women concerts; adjunct professor of songwriting at Lee University; television talk-show host of *Babbie's House*; and a published author. The parents of two adult sons, Babbie and her husband, Charles, live on a farm in West Georgia.

For more information, visit AbingdonPress.com, AbingdonWomen.com,
or your favorite Christian retailer.